VALLEY 1/24/2007
50690010
LeBouti
The story
 Knicks /

S0-GHT-442

VALLEY COMMUNITY LIBRARY
739 RIVER STREET
PECKVILLE, PA 18452
(570) 489-1765
www.lclshome.org

THE STORY OF THE
NEW YORK
KNICKS

CREATIVE EDUCATION

Published by Creative Education
123 South Broad Street
Mankato, Minnesota 56001
Creative Education is an imprint of The Creative Company.

DESIGN AND PRODUCTION BY **EVANSDAY DESIGN**

PHOTOGRAPHS BY Associated Press, AP, Getty Images (Nathaniel S. Butler / NBAE, Garrett Ellwood / NBAE, Jesse D. Garrabrant, Noah Graham / NBAE, Walter Looss Jr. / NBAE, Perry H. Kretz / Keystone Features, Mansell / Time Life Pictures, Fernando Medina / NBAE, Ken Regan / NBAE, Wen Roberts / NBAE, Jamie Squire / Allsport, Justin Sullivan, Noren Trotman / NBAE)

Copyright © 2007 Creative Education.
International copyright reserved in all countries.
No part of this book may be reproduced in any form
without written permission from the publisher.
Printed in the United States of America

LIBRARY OF CONGRESS CATALOGING-IN-PUBLICATION DATA

LeBoutillier, Nate.
The story of the New York Knicks / by Nate LeBoutillier.
p. cm. — (The NBA—a history of hoops)
Includes index.
ISBN-13: 978-1-58341-418-7
1. New York Knickerbockers (Basketball team)—History—
Juvenile literature. I. Title. II. Series.

GV885.52.N4L43 2006
796.323'64'097471—dc22   2005051786

First edition

9 8 7 6 5 4 3 2 1

COVER PHOTO: *Stephon Marbury*

NATE LeBOUTILLIER

CREATIVE EDUCATION

Just after 7:30

On the evening of May 8, 1970, New York Knicks center Willis Reed limped onto a basketball court for Game 7 of the National Basketball Association (NBA) Finals. What started as scattered shouting turned into a deafening roar from the Madison Square Garden crowd. Knicks guard Bill Bradley recalled: "We left the locker room for warm-ups not knowing if Willis was going to come out or not." Despite his leg injury, Reed scored the Knicks' first two baskets, inspiring his teammates to a 113–99 win and the Knicks' first NBA championship.

BASKETBALL, NEW YORK CITY STYLE

THE PULSE OF BASKETBALL HAS ALWAYS BEEN IN THE bounce of the ball, the iron clang of the rim, the swish of the net. As New York City rose to greater and greater prominence in America in the latter half of the 20th century, the lifeblood of the game of basketball flowed into the streets. Playgrounds in New York City have been where legends have been made, where the best of the best have come to showcase their game. It was only fitting, therefore, that the city of New York have a professional team that could effectively represent its basketball bloodlines.

In 1946, when the Basketball Association of America (BAA) was founded, New York fielded a team called the Knickerbockers, or Knicks. From the start, the Knicks established themselves as one of the classiest teams in

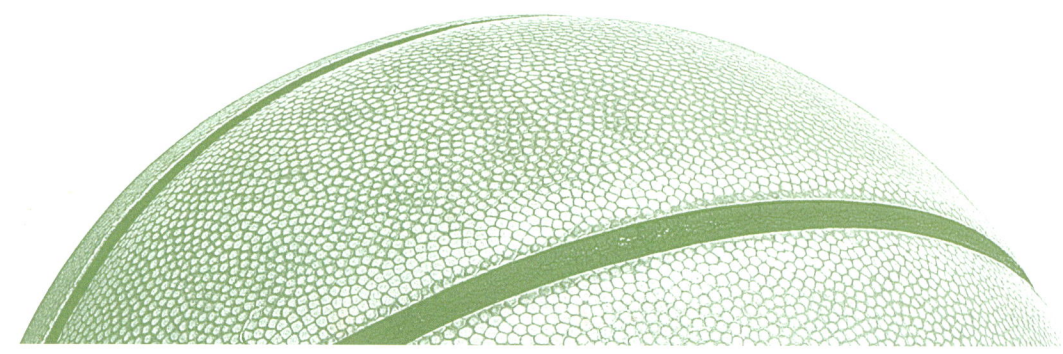

NEW YORK

KNICKS

Grounded in competition on the city's playground courts, New York's basketball roots run deep

HOOPS 1951

Carl Braun emerged as the Knicks' first star, a reliable 15-points-per-game scorer and a tenacious defender

the BAA and then in the NBA, which was formed three years later. Ned Irish, the club's founder, had a clear-cut philosophy. "We will create first-class conditions for a first-class team in a first-class city," he declared.

Irish also found a first-class coach to lead his new squad: Joe Lapchick, who left nearby St. John's University to take over the local pro team. Lapchick's reputation as a basketball genius helped him draw top young talent to the Knicks. In 1947, for example, Carl Braun—an outstanding baseball and basketball prospect—decided to break his contract with the New York Yankees just for the chance to play basketball under Lapchick. The young forward quickly became the Knicks' top offensive star.

Braun was joined in New York by center Harry Gallatin, guards Dick McGuire and Ernie "Doc" Vandeweghe, and forward Vince Boryla. These players, collectively known as the "New York Five," were small (no player stood taller than 6-foot-6) but lightning-quick, and they played great team basketball. The New York Five reached the NBA Finals in 1951, 1952, and 1953, but they were never quite able to bring home a championship trophy. Then, starting with the 1956–57 season, New York finished last in its division 9 out of 10 years and made the playoffs just once.

KNICKERBOCKERS NICKNAME

In 1626, a group of Dutch settlers purchased a small island along the middle Atlantic coast and called it New Amsterdam. These settlers wore special knee-length pants called "knickerbockers," or "knickers" for short. Less than 40 years later, the settlement was passed along to the British, who renamed it New York. Much of the city's Dutch heritage faded over the years, but the term "Knickerbocker" stayed alive and was used to describe any resident who could trace his or her ancestry back to the original settlers. "Father Knickerbocker" became the symbol of the city, especially in political cartoons. After New York was awarded an NBA franchise, its owners needed to pick a name for the club and put several suggestions in a hat. Knickerbockers was the name drawn out, and the New York Knicks were born.

HOLZMAN STEPS IN, KNICKS STEP UP

IN 1967, THE KNICKS HIRED WILLIAM "RED" HOLZMAN as their new coach. Holzman believed in team play, and under his direction, the Knicks drafted and traded for team-oriented players.

Six-foot-nine center Willis Reed, the club's captain and inspirational leader, was wide and strong, and he had the heart to outfight bigger players. Forwards Dave DeBusschere and Bill Bradley were tireless workers and good shots. Guard Walt Frazier proved to be an offensive *and* defensive stalwart, and swingman Dick Barnett was outstanding in the clutch. Coming off the bench were long-range bomber Cazzie Russell and defensive specialist Phil Jackson, a gangly forward who would later become one of the NBA's most successful coaches.

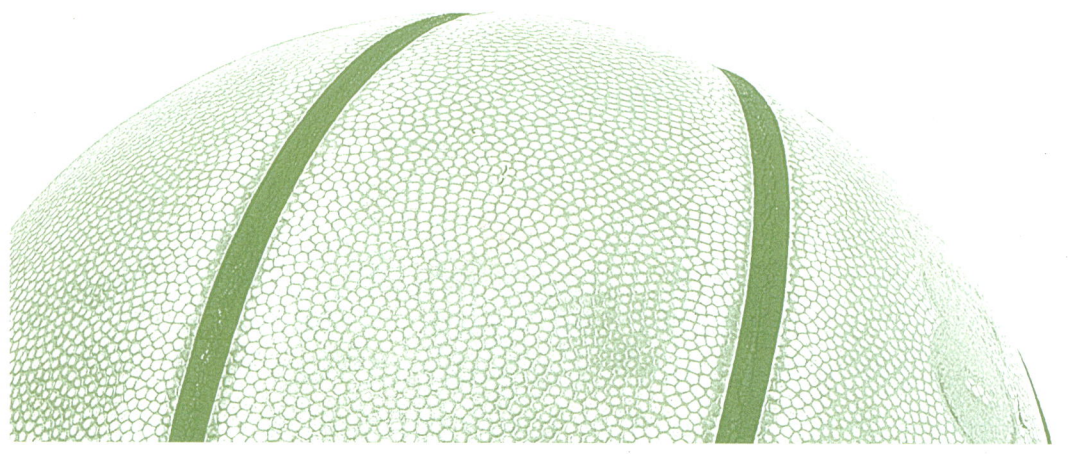

Although just 6-foot-6, Dave DeBusschere was nicknamed "Big D" because of his high-pressure defense

Holzman molded these individuals into an outstanding and unselfish unit. "It was a chemistry with the Knicks," said DeBusschere. "We found that when we got those lines of communication open, the willingness to sacrifice to help our team or teammates—not expecting anything in return—was a common goal."

In 1969–70, Holzman's team won a club-record 60 games and stormed through the first two rounds of the playoffs and into the NBA Finals. The Los Angeles Lakers stood in their way, led by future Hall-of-Famers Wilt Chamberlain, Jerry West, and Elgin Baylor. The teams split the first six games, but Reed sat out most of Games 5 and 6 with a thigh injury.

Just before Game 7 began, Reed decided to play despite his painful injury. "It was like getting your right arm sewed back on," said Cazzie Russell. The hometown fans went wild as Reed walked onto the court for the opening tip. In their hearts, the game and the championship were already won. Four quarters of basketball later, the Knicks had a 113–99 victory. After 23 years, the Knickerbockers were finally champions.

Three years later, the Knicks won a second title with a slightly different cast. Guard Earl "The Pearl" Monroe joined the team, and backing up Reed at center was future Hall-of-Famer Jerry Lucas. The Frazier-Monroe backcourt directed another balanced New York attack and propelled the Knicks to a four-games-to-one rout of the Lakers for the 1973 championship.

WALT "CLYDE" FRAZIER

Walt Frazier, number 10 for the New York Knicks, was a cool customer. Off the court, his flashy wardrobe and laid-back demeanor made him a hit in the city. On the court, "Clyde" was a ferocious defender whose quick feet and even quicker hands drove opponents crazy. In the 1970 Game 7 victory over the Los Angeles Lakers that gave the Knicks their first NBA championship, everyone remembers Willis Reed's valiant and inspirational comeback. But Reed *was* injured, and not able to play much in the game. Frazier, meanwhile, had 36 points, 19 assists, and 5 steals in one of his best games ever. But the Knicks played as a team, and Willis often gave credit to Frazier, once saying, "It's Clyde's ball. He just lets us play with it once in a while."

Phil Jackson (left) and Jerry Lucas (center) helped the Knicks top the Lakers for the 1973 NBA championship

NEW YORK KNICKS

KING, EWING, AND THE '80S

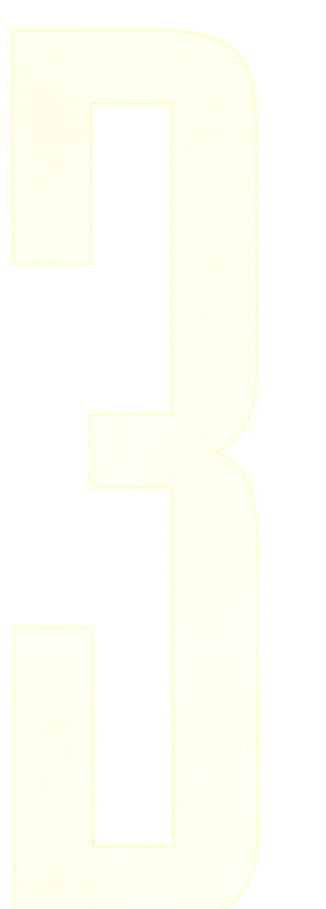

COACH HOLZMAN'S KNICKS COULD NOT EARN A THIRD title. One by one, the team's core players retired or were traded away. After the Knicks stumbled to a 33–49 record during the 1981–82 season, Holzman retired and was replaced by Hubie Brown.

It took the Knicks a while to adapt to Coach Brown's style, but they started winning again. One key reason for their success was the play of forward Bernard King, who arrived in New York in 1982. A fierce competitor, the 6-foot-7 King could hit consistently from the outside, but his specialty was driving inside. "Bernard has an incredibly explosive first step to the basket," said Coach Brown.

NEW YORK

SHOOTING

New York native Bernard King had rare scoring talent, netting an NBA-best 33 points a game in 1984–85

19

Big center Patrick Ewing was an 11-time All-Star and the face of the Knicks for a decade and a half

Unfortunately, King was injured early in the 1984–85 season, and the club sank in the standings. The Knicks' low finish that year gave them the top pick in the 1985 NBA Draft, and they used it on a player who would be the heart of the team for the next 15 years—center Patrick Ewing. "The Patrick Ewing Era Has Begun," a May 13, 1985, headline in *The New York Times* announced.

At Georgetown University, Ewing had led the Hoyas to three National Collegiate Athletic Association (NCAA) Final Four appearances, and the Knicks were counting on the 7-footer to lead them to glory as well. Ewing was a dominant presence in the paint and boasted a deadly fadeaway jump shot. He also had a brooding "game face" that intimidated opponents.

The Ewing era in New York got off to a rocky start. It took several years—and several coaching changes—before the Knicks generated some success. In the late '80s, they added guard Mark Jackson, power forward Charles Oakley, and shooting guard John Starks. These players led New York to a string of playoff appearances that started in 1988 and continued throughout the 1990s.

MADISON SQUARE GARDEN

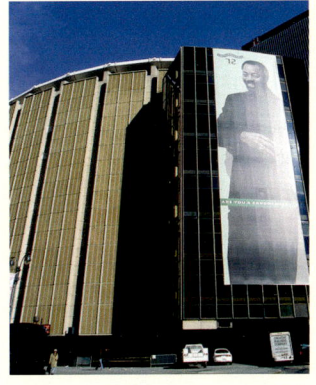

In the heart of Manhattan (a New York borough) is "The World's Most Famous Arena." Madison Square Garden, home of the Knicks, has hosted great basketball and important cultural events since 1879. There have actually been four Madison Square Gardens, with each renovation taking on qualities of the last. The current Garden was built in 1968 and has hosted such events as the Knicks' first NBA championship (in 1970), the 1971 Muhammad Ali-George Frazier title fight, and both Democratic and Republican political conventions. The Garden has also hosted scores of musical events, from the Beatles to Bruce Springsteen. "It doesn't matter if it's Michael Jordan, or Muhammad Ali, or Sinatra, or the pope," said George Kalinsky, the official Garden photographer for nearly 40 years. "They know the stage is brighter here than anyplace else."

NEAR-CHAMPIONSHIP YEARS

BEFORE THE 1991–92 SEASON, THE KNICKS ADDED A new coach—the legendary Pat Riley, who had guided the Lakers to four NBA championships during the 1980s. With Riley's pushing and prodding, the Knicks became one of the top teams in the NBA during his four years in New York. They reached the Eastern Conference Finals twice and the NBA Finals once in search of another title.

The Knicks' closest encounter with a championship came in the 1994 playoffs, when they grabbed a three-games-to-two NBA Finals lead over the Houston Rockets and needed just one more victory to claim the crown. It never came. Stellar play by the Rockets' gifted center, Hakeem Olajuwon, led to two heartbreaking defeats for the Knicks.

NEW YORK KNICKS

In four seasons under coach Pat Riley, New York went a combined 223–105 and made the playoffs every year

At a bruising 6-foot-7 and 240 pounds, Larry Johnson bolstered the Knicks' reputation for physical play

Riley left New York in 1995 to become coach of the Miami Heat and was replaced by assistant coach Jeff Van Gundy. The coaching shuffle was the first of many changes in New York in the late '90s. In a major face-lift, New York put forward Larry Johnson and guard Allan Houston in Knicks uniforms, as well as point guard Charlie Ward, swingman Latrell Sprewell, and high-flying center Marcus Camby. Through it all, the one consistent thread was Patrick Ewing.

Michael Jordan and the Chicago Bulls' six championships in the '90s had thwarted almost everyone else's NBA championship plans. But when Jordan retired in 1998, the Knicks took advantage. The 1998–99 Knicks barely made the playoffs but hit their stride in the postseason. First, New York shocked Coach Riley's top-seeded Miami Heat in the first round. The Knicks wiped out Atlanta in the next round, then took out Indiana in the Eastern Conference Finals. But Ewing was injured in the Indiana series, and New York's run was brought to a halt in the NBA Finals by the San Antonio Spurs.

In 2000, Knicks management made a major change, trading Patrick Ewing to Seattle. Ewing's departure after 15 years in New York was an emotional one. "Patrick is a champion, even if he hasn't won a championship," said Coach Van Gundy. "He practiced and played like a champion each day he was here."

Latrell Sprewell added speed to New York's offense, often streaking downcourt for fast-break scores

THE DUNK In Game 2 of the 1993 Eastern Conference Finals between New York and the hated Chicago Bulls, popular Knicks guard John Starks made a play for the ages. Known simply as "The Dunk" to most Knicks fans, the 6-foot-5 Starks leaped over both the 6-foot-10 Horace Grant and the 6-foot-6, high-flying Michael Jordan to dunk the ball with his left hand (Starks was right-handed). The dunk came with time running down and helped the Knicks win the game. "I was never intimidated to go inside against the big guys," said Starks, known for his scrappy style. "That's part of the game. The way I looked at it, I've been playing against bigger guys all my life—even on the playground growing up as a little fellow."

THE KNICKERBOCKERS TODAY

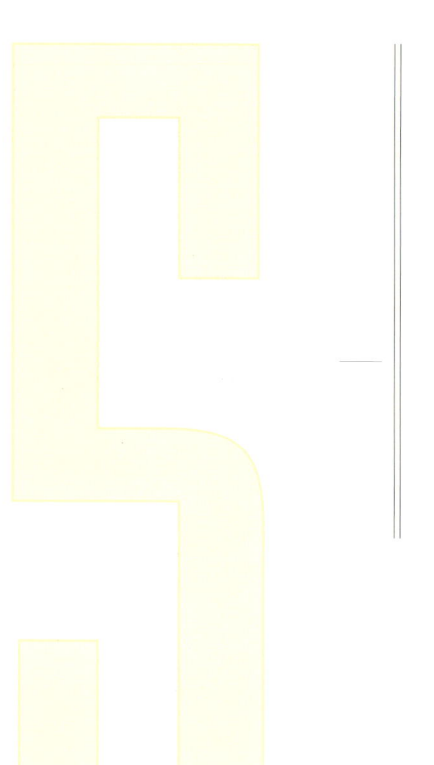

IN 2001–02, THE KNICKS FELL TO 30–52, AND THREE losing seasons followed. Former Detroit Pistons star Isiah Thomas took over as team president in 2003. One of Thomas's first moves was to engineer a trade bringing home Coney Island, New York, native Stephon Marbury to play the point guard position. To help Marbury, Thomas also traded for talented guard Jamal Crawford.

NEW YORK

KNICKS

Famous for his explosive quickness, Stephon Marbury was acquired as part of New York's rebuilding efforts

29

HOOPS 811

New York fans counted on rising guard Jamal Crawford to help the Knicks capture that elusive third title

In 2005, the Knicks continued to reload by selecting University of Arizona center Channing Frye, a 7-footer with a soft shooting touch. But a bigger move was the hiring of NBA coaching great and New York City native Larry Brown, who would be called upon to inject discipline into a motley Knicks lineup. "I grew up on a playground where if you lost, you went to the back of the line and wouldn't play for a while," Brown said, illustrating his coaching style. "And if you took a bad shot, one of the bigger guys would crack you."

For more than half a century, the New York Knicks have lived up to founder Ned Irish's vision of "a first-class team in a first-class city." Loyal New York fans who witnessed Willis Reed's valiant leadership in 1970 have come to expect that kind of excellent basketball in Madison Square Garden. With a new coach from the old streets of New York City, today's Knicks plan to deliver.

SUPERFAN SPIKE LEE

Every team has its famous fans, and Spike Lee is the Knicks'. As a filmmaker and occasional actor, Lee has created many movies, including the basketball-themed *He Got Game*. Lee is also famous for playing Michael Jordan's sidekick, Mars Blackmon, in Nike shoe commercials starting in the 1980s. But what set him apart as a Knicks fan were the many shouting matches he got into from his courtside seat in Madison Square Garden with opposing players, especially Indiana Pacers star Reggie Miller. "I was eight years old when I started attending basketball games at the old Garden with my dad, and we sat upstairs in the nosebleed seats," said Lee, remembering his first Knicks experiences. "That's all we could afford, and that was fine with us."

INDEX

B

Barnett, Dick 12
Basketball Association of America 8, 11
Boryla, Vince 11
Bradley, Bill 5, 12
Braun, Carl **10**, 11
Brown, Hubie 18
Brown, Larry 31

C

Camby, Marcus 25
Crawford, Jamal 28, **30**

D

DeBusschere, Dave 12, **13**, 15

E

Ewing, Patrick **20**, 21, 25

F

Frazier, Walt ("Clyde") 12, **14**, 16, **16**
Frye, Channing 31

G

Gallatin, Harry 11

H

Holzman, William ("Red") 12, 15, 18
Houston, Allan 25

I

Irish, Ned 11, 31

J

Jackson, Mark 21
Jackson, Phil 12, **16–17**
Johnson, Larry **24**, 25

K

King, Bernard 18, **19**, 21

L

Lapchick, Joe 11
Lee, Spike 31, **31**
Lucas, Jerry 15, **16–17**

M

Madison Square Garden 5, 21, **21**, 31
Marbury, Stephon 28, **29**
McGuire, Dick 11
Monroe, Earl ("The Pearl") 15

N

NBA championship 5, 15, 16
NBA Finals 5, 11, 15, 16, 22, 25
NBA playoffs 5, 11, 15, 16, 21, 22, 25, 27
"New York Five" 11
New York Knicks
    name 11
    team record 15

O

Oakley, Charles 21

R

Reed, Willis **4**, 5, 12, 15, 16, 31
Riley, Pat 22, **23**, 25
Russell, Cazzie 12, 15

S

Sprewell, Latrell 25, **26–27**
Starks, John 21, 27, **27**

T

Thomas, Isiah 28

V

Van Gundy, Jeff 25
Vandeweghe, Ernie ("Doc") 11

W

Ward, Charlie 25